Bibliographic information published by the German National Library:

The German National Library lists this publication in the National Bibliography; detailed bibliographic data are available on the Internet at http://dnb.dnb.de .

Imprint:

Copyright © 2013 GRIN Verlag, Open Publishing GmbH
Print and binding: Books on Demand GmbH, Norderstedt Germany
ISBN: 9783656485919

This book at GRIN:

http://www.grin.com/en/e-book/231593/are-kevin-bales-suggestions-for-reforming-the-united-nations-so-as-to

Georg Müller

Aus der Reihe: e-fellows.net stipendiaten-wissen

e-fellows.net (Hrsg.)

Band 775

Are Kevin Bales' suggestions for reforming the United Nations so as to bring the end of slavery too idealistic?

Reconsidering the importance of the UN

GRIN Publishing

GRIN - Your knowledge has value

Since its foundation in 1998, GRIN has specialized in publishing academic texts by students, college teachers and other academics as e-book and printed book. The website www.grin.com is an ideal platform for presenting term papers, final papers, scientific essays, dissertations and specialist books.

Visit us on the internet:

http://www.grin.com/

http://www.facebook.com/grincom

http://www.twitter.com/grin_com

Are Kevin Bales' suggestions for reforming the United Nations so as to bring the end of slavery too idealistic? - Reconsidering the importance of the UN

Today slavery is not only officially illegal in all nations but furthermore every human being has, in reversion, a non-derogable right not to be enslaved thus giving the crime of slavery a jus cogens status. Nonetheless, together with other jus cogens norms such as the prohibition of torture or genocide, slavery still prevails in the world with unprecedented numbers of modern slaves. Kevin Bales claims, however, that the UN together with other transnational organizations can potentially contribute to ending slavery rather sooner than later – if they are reformed. This paper will focus on his arguments for reforming the UN and its associated organizations so as to achieve this goal. It will argue that while Bales makes a very good case for reforming the UN his propositions seem sometimes only to have aspirational character and it appears questionable whether they can ever be implemented. However, this is not to say that his suggestions are not of tremendous importance, but rather, this essay wants to argue that the importance of the UN should not be overstated. Generally this essay will focus first on whether the reforms suggested by Bales are feasible and second if they are to be implemented how effective they can be in eradicating slavery. Regarding the first point this essay will outline different arguments regarding the implementation of the reforms according to Slaughter's and Mearsheimer's line of argumentation. In regard to the latter point this essay will focus first on the lack of enforceability while acknowledging the informational power of the UN and second on the underlying problems of slavery that stand to some extend in contrast to the UN's mission. Finally this paper will conclude that while it is not impossible to implement the proposed changes in the UN there are considerable challenges to be overcome and furthermore the effect these changes might have on the process of abolishing slavery might be rather small.

Bales outlines a five point plan, which the UN, including the Security Council, should implement to effectively fight slavery: first, appoint a special representative of the secretary-general on slavery; second hold a Security Council meeting on the matter of slavery; third make significant contributions to the budget of the special representative; fourth appoint a committee of experts to review slavery conventions and fifth determine how to expand the UN inspection mandate to slavery (Bales, 174). On first sight these steps seem quite straightforward; however, considering the complexity of competing interests within the UN as well as its bureaucratic structure it seems anything but simple to achieve these goals. It is undoubtedly true that the state is still the most important actor in international issues and the UN represents the interests of those countries; although power is very much skewed. Furthermore it is true that slavery exists in every country in the world no matter how developed it is. If one accepts these premises one needs to ask, keeping Mearsheimer's theory in mind, why countries should make any additional efforts in abolishing slavery. Economically slaves present only a small fraction of the population, especially in Western countries. In European countries slaves constitute mostly less than 0.5% of the population according to recent extrapolation estimates by Datta and Bales (21). There is no doubt that holding any person prisoner through the use of physical or psychological force is a heinous crime that needs to be prosecuted; however, the political and economic reality seems to suggest that the abolition of slavery often comes second or third to other interests of the state. With this in mind it seems not surprising that it took the German government, which is certainly considered a very liberal and democratic legislative branch, over six years to ratify a European convention on the fight against slavery and human trafficking due to concerns about migration control (3sat.de). These policy lags in national legislative cast some doubts on whether such changes are feasible on the international level, where multiple state interests collide. On the other hand is not true anymore that states only act as a unit but rather can the increasing importance of transnational networks be observed.

2

One should not underestimate the fact that states are not purely acting as unitary states, but there also exist, following the argument by Slaughter, many transnational networks that begin to operate within international organizations such as the UN or the NATO (106). This development can potentially lead to a more just and less state-centric decision making process, at least if it comes to matters of international crime. No state, at least not officially, denies the necessity to abolish slavery, but hardly any nation acts by rigorously enforcing anti-slavery laws. On this basis a developing governmental network that is truly concerned about the issue of slavery might therefore be able to overcome the barriers that prevented states from acting and might actually be able to implement the suggested reforms with the goal of eradicating slavery. For Western states the push in this direction, it seems, needs to come from the public, since economic incentives are too low to push for action on this topic. Although the USA has passed already under Bill Clinton a law threatening sanctions against countries that do not actively engage in anti-slavery operations, the political reality was that only states, which were not strategically important to the US, were actually sanctioned. Any attempts to try to sanction Japan with its 120,000 sex slaves or the Arabic Emirates were immediately denied (3sat.de). Therefore public pressure is crucial to move the political process forward. But even if the UN can be reformed as suggested by Bales it is not necessarily obvious if and in how far these changes can make a difference.

Bales suggest, among other things, the extension of the UN inspectors mandate as well the adaption of slavery law into international law thus making countries and people theoretically responsible before the International Court of Justice and the International Criminal Court, respectively. However, it is important to note that firstly, the jurisdiction of the courts is anything but undisputed and secondly, their effectiveness has so far not been very high, with them only handling a small amount of cases and very long trial periods. Even after these proposed changes would be implemented, there would have to be UN inspectors in every country on a regular basis, which is not only an expensive and time consuming endeavor, but furthermore will it be difficult to actually observe the prevalence of slavery in every country. After all slavery is not a large governmental program on the scale of building weapons of mass destruction or enriching uranium, but rather a widely dispersed phenomenon observable in all layers of the society and often obscured by pseudo-legal contracts. These factors should make it inherently difficult to observe the accurate compliance of countries to anti-slavery standards. However, it might be argued that the presence of UN inspectors can still have considerable effects on certain countries that want to protect their political status worldwide. It should be kept in mind, however, that those actions largely depend on the country's cooperation. Bales argues appropriately that countries certainly do not want to risk more or less severe economic and political sanctions just to protect their slavery business (154). But even then, once the problem has been to some extend identified in all countries, it is questionable how the UN wants to make the step from the knowledge about the prevalence of slavery to enforceable legal statutes that can and will be applied nationally. However, maybe the UN does not necessarily need to try to enforce a legislative top-down approach but should rather focus on its informal power.

It should not be neglected that international institutions can have significant effects, without necessary having to be able to enforce any legislation. Koehane argues for the power of those organizations, such as the UN, in terms of their informational status (43). It is true that the UN has certain powers derived from multilateral treaties and can use their global reach and internal structure to start a process of change. Ad hoc and permanent working groups can produce influential reports to create political and even economic pressure, if the Security Council gets involved. When criticizing Bales this paper is aware that the main approach of the UN in general and the Office of the High Commissioner for Human Rights (OHCHR) in particular is one based on information and advocacy. In this respect the ILO's and UN's eradication project of child slavery in the mining and quarrying sector in some 15 countries through advocacy projects and ultimately an education and vocational training as well as an alternative livelihood scheme, helped eradicate slavery in the sector almost entirely (Shahinian, 18). However, these success stories must also not conceal that the UN's power is largely dependent on other countries' cooperation. While a special representative on slavery as well as an increased publicity effort would certainly raise awareness under the population in many states, one needs to be clear about the actual extend of these actions. It cannot be denied that publicity efforts are most effective there, where a strong civil society exists – which is mostly true only for the Western world. As established earlier, slavery is truly a global phenomenon; however, it also is most prevalent in developing and underdeveloped countries with a weak government, as well as civil society. This leads to the conclusion that there must exist other factors worth considering when thinking about how to utilize international organizations in the fight against slavery.

It is important that Bales addresses not only the changes necessary within the UN office particularly responsible for fighting slavery, namely the OHCHR, but also other UN organizations such as the WHO, FAO, UNESCO or the UN Peace Corps, because those address the underlying causes of slavery. These worldwide issues, such as poverty, education, corruption or health, this essay argues, are quintessential in overcoming slavery. Especially if the effectiveness of transnational anti-slavery conventions is in doubt it appears crucial to focus on those issues that ultimately cause slavery. Although official development assistance (ODA) to fight poverty is a highly debated topic it is undoubtedly true that there exists a far wider network and knowledge base for the fight against poverty than for the fight against slavery, where little research has been carried out so far. Therefore maybe the UN should shift more expertise and funds to the fight against the underlying problems of slavery than to the fight against slavery itself. This is not to say that there should be no funding for and further research into the fight against slavery – on the contrary this is crucial to exactly understand the factors causing it – but considering the reluctance of states to seriously attack the issue, it might be more effective to focus on those underlying issues. This argument is, of course, highly susceptible to criticism on the grounds that lastly many of the world's problems can be traced back to poverty and therefore we do not need to focus on anything else; however, this essay would like to emphasize that the issue of slavery is in so far different as the national interest in overcoming it is worldwide rather marginal. National interest in abolishing slavery is ultimately crucial to its success; but not only if this interest is expressed in the international context but more importantly if sincere actions are undertaken on a domestic level.

Addressing the challenges of the UN by strict reforms cannot do much in changing national legislation or even the demand for slaves. Every effective strategy that wants to abolish slavery necessarily needs to deal with the two parts of slavery: supply and demand. While the supply issue contains both the problems that forces people into slavery, such as poverty or abduction and the problems that enable people to escape slavery and stay free (after-care) the demand site contains all those factors and moral norms under which people are trafficked for sale, are enslaved for economic exploitation or held as sex slaves. It seems that this site can only be addressed very insufficiently by the UN. However, it is possible to focus on this site more intensely through vigorous and extensive marketing campaigns, which might raise awareness, but of course suffer from the flaws mentioned earlier. In this respect this essay argues that Bales could have addressed this issue more intensively. To better illustrate the problems associated with the demand site of slavery this essay wants to provide several examples. One of the largest issues in the opinion of this author is "simply" capitalism, expressed in the demand for cheap products, the constant drive for growth and ruthless market competition. One campaign lead by a large chain of electronic stores in Germany a few years ago is exemplary for this. The Saturn electronic stores as part of the Media-Saturn-Holding GmbH advertised for many years with the slogan "Geiz ist Geil" ("Stinginess is sexy") (Spiegel.de). This slogan serves to some extend as a summary of the consumer behavior in the free market economy. While Bales discusses the aspects of supply chain management and international trade in relation to slavery, any reform of the UN can only in so far address slavery as it can incentivize countries to change national legislation and enforce those laws rigorously. It seems doubtful whether this will be truly effective as long as the public perception as well as consumer behavior does not shift significantly.

In conclusion this paper showed that there are good reasons for doubting whether Bales' suggestions can realistically be implemented. Nonetheless this paper argued that Bales' ideas are important for starting a process of change in the UN and among the population. However, this essay also pointed out that the actual influence of the UN in abolishing slavery should not be overstated as there exist many underlying issues that cannot be sufficiently addressed by the UN. At the same time this paper established that it appears to be far easier to eradicate slavery in those countries that possess a strong civil society, namely Western countries. Consequently this paper also concludes that policy-advocacy campaigns for the true abolition of slavery should be vastly intensified in the Western world. This could not only cause those countries to change, but could also have a spillover effect to developing countries, once Western countries reach this goal. This paper realizes that any attempt on the international level to motivate countries to take further actions to eradicate slavery will be very difficult. However, Bales' suggestions are without a doubt as necessary as they are ambitious.

Bibliography

3sat.de. 2011. "Moderne Sklaverei." September 15.
http://www.3sat.de/page/?source=/scobel/155547/index.htmlid18712236.html
(accessed March 07, 2013).

Bales, Kevin. 2007. *Ending Slavery. How we free today's slaves.* Berkeley: University
of California Press.

Datta, M., Bales, K. 2013. "Estimating Modern Day Slavery. An Empirical Analsysis of
37 European Countries." Unpublished.

Keohane, Robert O., Martin, Lisa L. 1995. "The Promise of Institutionalist Theory."
International Security 20 (1): 39-51. JSTOR (January 25, 2013).

Mearsheimer, John T. 1995. "The False Promise of International Institutions."
International Security 19 (3): 5-49. JSTOR (January 25, 2013).

Shahinian, G. 2011. "Report of the Special Rapporteur on contemporary forms of
slavery, including its causes and consequences." [online] Available at:
http://www.ohchr.org/Documents/Issues/Slavery/SR/A-HRC-18-30_en.pdf (accessed
March 07, 2013).

Slaughter, Anne-Marie. 2006. *A New World Order.* Oxfordshire: Princeton University
Press.

Spiegel.de. 2007. "Werbeslogans: geiz war geil." May 29.
http://www.spiegel.de/wirtschaft/werbeslogans-geiz-war-geil-a-485489.html
(accessed March 07, 2013).